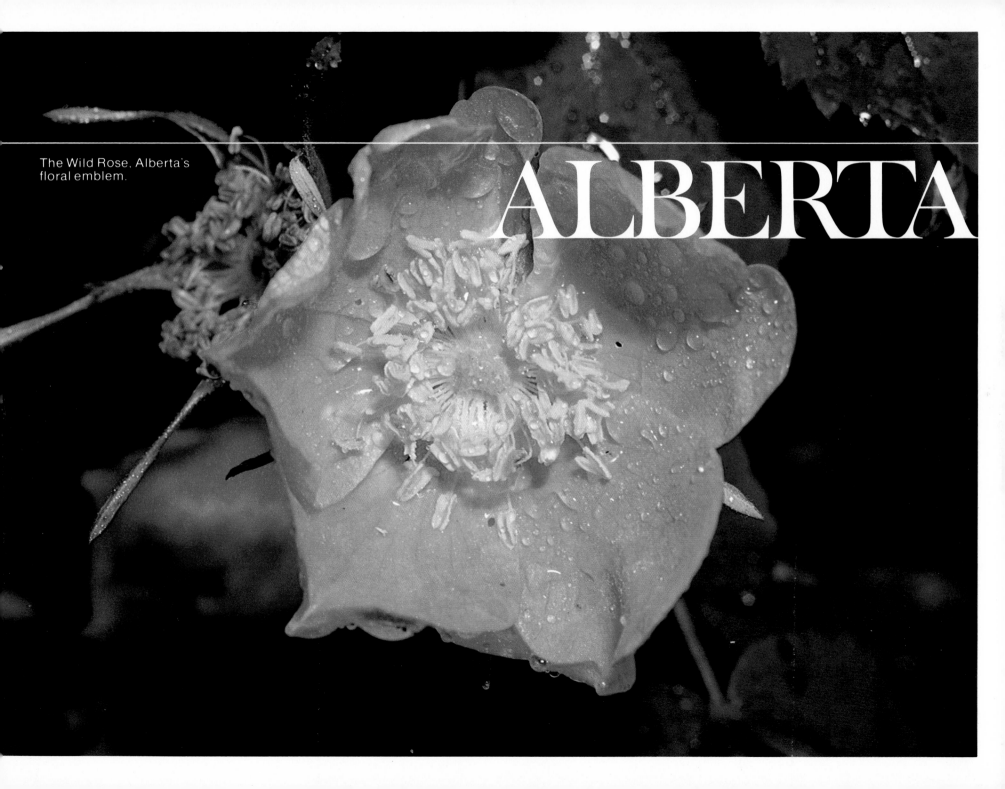

The Wild Rose, Alberta's
floral emblem.

ALBERTA

A grain elevator at Calmar
glows golden in the rays of a
Prairie sunset.

ALBERTA

This book is dedicated to
Ken Okura
Gardener, Fisherman, Philosopher

Text and photographs by Bill Brooks,
with the exception of Klondike Days
(Ron Kearney/Edmonton Klondike
Days Association) and Roughnecks
(Barry Dursley/Imperial Oil Limited).

Photographer, author: Bill Brooks

Designer: René Demers
Craib Demers Associates Limited

Editor: John Robert Colombo

Publisher: Anthony Hawke

Printer: Heritage Press

Hounslow Press
A Division of Anthony R. Hawke Limited
124 Parkview Avenue
Willowdale, Ontario, Canada M2N 3Y5

Printed in Canada

Beef cattle graze in the
shadow of the Rocky
Mountains near Ghost Lake.

A big land, bustling, brawling, oil-rich, growing by leaps and bounds, long on jobs, short on pollution, bursting the bonds of an old economy heavily dependent on Eastern interests, Alberta is the new Promised Land.

A teenager of a province, Alberta has all the gusto, plans, dreams, sexuality, ambitions, and reckless courage of youth. Here people have the lean frames that come from good, honest toil in the fields, on the oil rigs, and in the saddle. None of your welfare flab here.

Permanent settlers first came with the railway in the 1880's, and yet, even today, there is still land open to homesteaders. The pioneer spirit remains close to the surface in Alberta. With the exception of the native population, all Albertans trace their roots to somewhere else, and even "old" families do not go back beyond the fourth or fifth generation.

All of this has left the province with a tremendously optimistic sense of tomorrow. Albertans feel they are just starting out on a great adventure. Society is free, the slate is clean, and hard-working men and women have a real chance to shoot for the top. They are not fenced in by history, by past decisions, or by the dry rot of upper-classmanship as are older and more sedate societies.

The pioneers, the ancestors of today's oil-lucky Albertans, faced their first cold Prairie winter with little more than a sod shack, a few turnips, and the will to survive. In a sense, the later discovery of oil is a return on investment for all those hardy settlers who had the guts to gamble their lives in an unknown land. Today, the sons and daughters of those courageous people are going to make sure that the hard-earned reward of oil will not be spent unwisely.

Not long ago, coal was the big resource in Alberta. It provided jobs and some money, but the bottom caved in, and there was nothing left to show for the resource that had only fueled the fires of industries elsewhere. A trip through the coal-mining ghost towns on the eastern slopes of the Rockies will go a long way towards explaining to an outsider the value Albertans place on their oil reserves.

Alberta has something for everyone. Do you want to be a pioneer? Then go North, for the top half of the province is virtually uninhabited. How about the sophistication of Calgary, or the hustle of Edmonton? If the life of a mountainman is more appealing, then go to the western edge of the province and commune with nature. The traditional Western life of cowboys punching cows while riding the dusty range is still preserved in the south.

I like Alberta. I like to shop windows on Calgary's Eighth Avenue Mall or Edmonton's McCaully Plaza. I like the excitement of a rodeo held in a small Peace River town, or the quiet solitude and sense of space under the giant dome of a Prairie sky. I like the sense of wonder at seeing a wild animal in its natural mountain environment. I like the high expectations so characteristic of the oil business. I like the cocky, optimistic feeling Albertans have that West is Best. I like being on the verge of even better things, for Alberta is plainly "where it's at."

Mount Chephren is re-
flected in Waterfowl Lake in
Banff National Park.

Canoes, backpacks, and
camping vans are a common
sight on Banff's main street.

Mount Rundle and the
Vermilion Lakes are only a
short walk from the Banff
townsite.

Snow is plentiful and
adventuresome skiers have
the mountain to themselves.

Hikers brave the cold winds
blowing off the Columbia
Icefield.

Peyto Lake proudly bears the name of the old-time mountain-man, Bill Peyto.

Fresh snow powders
the trees at the summit of
Sulphur Mountain.

A chill wind ripples the
surface of glacier-fed Bow
Lake.

The Angel Glacier hangs
on the slopes of Mount Edith
Cavell.

The Athabasca River rush-
es past the cloud-draped
mountains.

From the vantage point of Bear's Hump, one can look along Waterton Lake to the International Border.

The ramparts of Mount
Eisenhower overlook the
Bow River.

Silent forests rim Lake
Louise.

A tour boat cruises un-
der snow-covered peaks at
Maligne Lake.

Tourists examine the
Athabasca Glacier where
the ice is 335 metres thick.

Bare Mountain glows in the
last light of day.

Running water exposes
layers of ancient rock in Red
Rock Canyon.

Mountain Creek makes
three separate drops
to traverse the Punchbowl
Falls.

Edmonton, the provincial capital, is the fast-growing nerve centre of the North.

The Alberta Legislative
Building stands on the site
of old Fort Edmonton.

The vaulted dome of the
Legislative Building soars
55 metres above the foun-
tain in the spectacular main
rotunda.

Modern art and traditional
Western headgear are seen
outside the Edmonton Art
Gallery.

Edmonton's city hall
overlooks the flowers of
Churchill Square.

Oil fuels the economy today, and nowhere is this fact more evident than along "refinery row" on Edmonton's eastern limits.

Edmonton was the last stop
on the trek to the Klondike
Gold Fields in 1898; this is
what Edmontonians recall
each summer when they
celebrate Klondike Days.

The Hub, a student residence at the University of Alberta, contains an indoor street complete with restaurants and stores.

The Alberta Telephone Tower looms over businessmen on their way to lunch at The Edmonton Club.

A restored Indian vil-
lage stands today in Fort
Edmonton Park.

University students, dressed
as the North West Mounted
Police, parade at the
restored Fort Macleod.

The Mounties chased the
whiskey traders out of the
Cypress Hills, and later more
sedate settlers built this
small church.

Colourful leaves and snow in
the Rockies signify fall in the
foothills near Cochrane.

The Red Deer River has
created the badlands of
Dinosaur Provincial Park.

Near Drumheller, wind
and water have carved
these weird shapes called
"hoodoos."

The Nikka Yuko Japanese
Garden in Lethbridge is an
oasis of peace in a bustling
Prairie city.

Dominated by grain elevators, the main street of Fairview is like many small towns in the Peace River Country.

The grave of Crowfoot, great
chief of the Blackfoot,
overlooks this scene near
Cluny.

Huge pumps bring oil to the
surface in a field near Tilley.

Mobile homes provide a
quick place to live for coal
miners in the frontier town of
Grande Cache.

Red Deer is a mostly new
city that burst the bonds of
the valley that contained the
original town.

The McDougall Church at
Morley has hardly changed
since it was established by
George McDougall in 1875.

A long double-engined train works its way across the flat, never-ending Prairie.

Icons of another age grace
the walls of the first Greek
Orthodox Church in Alberta,
now moved to the Shandro
Museum near Willingdon.

The world's largest
Ukrainian Easter Egg is on
display at Vegreville.

Medicine Hat occupies the
tree-filled valley of the South
Saskatchewan River.

Evening showers move
above summer homes on
Chestermere Lake.

Wheat grows as far as the
eye can see.

Clouds cast their shadows
over the rolling Prairie near
Milk River.

Lines of steel shoot across
an almost-infinite plain.

Roughnecks drill for oil in
Alberta's frozen North.

Beef cattle await the
inevitable in the Calgary
stockyards.

Headquarters of the oil in-
dustry; new buildings seem
to sprout up overnight in
booming bustling Calgary.

The bold architecture of the
New West mixes with the
Old along Calgary's Eighth
Avenue Mall.

Conventioneers take in the
sights on a stroll along the
Mall.

Devonian Gardens, an
indoor public park, takes the
sting out of Western winters.

The Glenbow Alberta
Institute documents the
history of the Canadian
west.

Lawn bowlers contest a
game on a quiet Sunday
afternoon.

Time out for some quiet
conversation at Calgary's
Heritage Park.

The chuckwagon race was invented at the Calgary Stampede and now it is a feature of rodeos everywhere.

This bareback rider, at a
rodeo in High Prairie,
managed to stay on his
horse.

Loggers show their skill, or
lack of it, at a competition in
Grande Prairie.

A mountain goat surveys
its vast domain from a cliff
overlooking the mighty
Athabasca River.

Bears are a common sight along roadsides, and woe betide the visitor who rolls down his window.

A curious mule deer
interrupts its feeding to
check some mysterious
sounds.

The wary cougar inhabits
the most remote regions.

A coyote follows the scent of
game along a forest trail.

The Gray Jay will often
visit picnic sites in search of
food.

The Clark's Nutcracker
looks down from a lofty
perch.

Bison are now found only in a few scattered pre-serves; these young were in Elk Island National Park.

This mother moose is contemplating a charge to protect her two young calves.

The hoary marmot spends its time in the rockfalls of the high mountains.

The scolding chirp of the Columbian ground squirrel can be heard in mountain meadows.

The male bighorn sheep leads a bachelor life in the summer but rejoins the herd in the fall.

Young bighorn lambs are
defended by their mothers.

An elk feeds on grasses in a
roadside meadow.

The sun sets on fishermen
trying their luck in Lac La
Biche.

Bill Brooks has been deeply involved with photographing the natural beauty of Canada and with the production of illustrated books since his graduation from the University of Toronto in 1962. He acquired his initial photographic experience as the manager of a well-known portrait studio and as the technical representative of a major camera and film manufacturer.

As photo editor for McClelland & Stewart from 1967 to 1972, he was involved in the creation of fine, illustrated books. It was during this period, while working on books extolling the wonders of Canada, that he realized, like most Canadians, just how little he knew about his own country.

He set out on a journey of discovery in 1972, with the hope of finding both the real Canada and his place in it. Since then he has produced: *Canada in Colour* (1972), *Ottawa: A Portrait of the Nation's Capital* (1973), *The Mill* (1976), *Wildlife of Canada* (1976), *The Colour of Ontario* (1977). And now, *The Colour of Alberta*.

Today, Bill Brooks' photographs of Canadian scenes are well-known, widely distributed, and frequently requested by major book and magazine publishers throughout the world ... thereby allowing him time in which to continue his journey of discovery.